More Boding than Blood

More Boding than Blood

Poems by

Don Gutteridge

First Edition

Hidden Brook Press
www.HiddenBrookPress.com
writers@HiddenBrookPress.com

More Boding than Blood
by Don Gutteridge

Cover Design – Richard M. Grove
Cover Image – Folly Media/Shutterstock, used by permission.
Layout and Design – Richard M. Grove

Typeset in Garamond
Printed and bound in Canada
Distributed in USA by Ingram,
            in Canada by Hidden Brook Distribution

Library and Archives Canada Cataloguing in Publication

Title: More boding than blood / poems by Don Gutteridge.
Names: Gutteridge, Don, 1937- author.
Identifiers: Canadiana (print) 20210211822 |
            Canadiana (ebook) 20210211830 |
            ISBN 9781989786413 (softcover) |
            ISBN 9781989786420 (ebook)
Classification: LCC PS8513.U85 M67 2021 |
            DDC C811/.54—dc23

Table of Contents

– More Boding than Blood – *p. 1*

– Hide and Seek – *p. 2*

– Holy – *p. 3*

– Pastoral – *p. 4*

– Bejewelled – *p. 5*

– Remembrance – *p. 6*

– Beyond Hope – *p. 7*

– When I Was Young Enough – *p. 8*

– The Knack – *p. 9*

– Ode – *p. 10*

– Festooned – *p. 11*

– The Breath in the Breeze – *p. 12*

– Budding – *p. 13*

– Heft – *p. 14*

– O What a Morning – *p. 15*

– Woo – *p. 16*

– Rhyme – *p. 17*

– Instinct – *p. 18*

– Cradle – *p. 19*

– A-Dazzle – *p. 20*

– Lost – *p. 21*

– Pouch – *p. 22*

– Far to Go – *p. 23*

– Scenery – *p. 24*

– Plots and Perils – *p. 25*

– The Morning of the World – *p. 26*

– Where Love Lives – *p. 27*

– Flock – *p. 28*

– Ruptured – *p. 29*

– Kingdom Come – *p. 30*

– Blinding – *p. 31*

Eight for Anne
In loving memory

– Linked – *p. 33*
– Illume – *p. 34*
– Autumn Morning: 1960 – *p. 35*
– Far Out – *p. 36*
– Winnowed – *p. 37*
– Gloaming – *p. 38*
– Serendipity – *p. 39*
– Lissome – *p. 40*

Sixteen for Tom
In Loving Memory

– Peaceful – *p. 42*
– Delirium – *p. 43*
– Similes – *p. 44*
– Immaculate – *p. 45*
– A Kind of Joy – *p. 46*
– Glee – *p. 47*
– Autumnal Wind – *p. 48*
– Something of Winter – *p. 49*
– More than Broken – *p. 50*
– Sally – *p. 51*
– All the Days – *p. 52*
– Lexicon – *p. 53*
– Radiant – *p. 54*
– Rhythms – *p. 55*
– Sweat – *p. 56*
– Eyrie – *p. 57*

– Author Biographical Note – *p. 59*

More Boding than Blood

For Tom in loving memory

If you had lived but one
more day, I would have walked you
into the milkweed meadow
where butterflies unbutton
their wings to bask on the breeze
and puckered pods, lanced
by light, expose their silken
sofas and larks sweeten
the air with saccharine song
and grasshoppers fling
free of gravity on tiny
trapezes and puff-adders
sputter loud enough
to frighten the frogs holidaying
on the pond and bulrushes
fluff their rusted coiffures –
and you would have said,
"So this is where the poems
gave birth to themselves?"
and I would reply, "Here
and in the kind of love
you brought me, more boding
than blood, more basic
than bone."

Hide and Seek

Under a night-sky
starved of stars with a moon
pruned to a sliver of silver
uneclipsed by cloud,
we loiter aloud below
the amber oval of Mara's
lamp, darting into the
larcenous dark just
to let the shiver of it
whet the appetite, and soon
we are cloaked in shadow and slyly
gendered (our hopes erotic):
lips nipping lips, a palm
impatient upon an unintended
knee, but the "All free!"
like the cry from a goitered
throat, draws us, like awed
moths, back to the ligature
of Mara's lambent light.

Holy

My Gran was chary of churching
but she tithed Anglican just
in case, and observed the Sabbath
by thinking of her maker as she kneaded
dough and scythed apples
for the pies she offered to those
she loved most, and I
was ever the first to sample
the merchandise, remembering
to thank the Father, the Son
and the Holy Ghost.

Pastoral

When I was a budding five,
Grandfather's lawn
rolled before me like the
ocean God gave to Noah
and his ark with its bellyful of beasts
or, when the sun simmered on it,
the Sea of Galilee that Jesus
sauntered his sandals on,
and the hedges that held the waters in
were lissome with lilacs that drooped
in languid loops, and further,
where islands idled, a brace
of maple trees, brushed
lush by a teasing breeze
and below that belled umbrella
grasses danced in dappled
delirium, and I was young
enough to float freely
in my bones, and roamed these
pastoral desmesnes as if
they were hearth and home.

Bejewelled

I was weaned on Bible stories:
Adam and Eve cavorting
in the Garden, naughtily nude,
but, alas, raddled by an adder;
Delilah, lopping hubby's
locks and cheering as the temple
columns toppled; David
and the potent pebble that felled
a giant; Daniel at ease
in the lion's den; Moses
in the bulrushes, tucked in wicker,
then commandeering Commandments,
weathering a wilderness and cleaving
a sea; Elijah, chuffed
with God and cruising moonward;
Zacharias in his trembling
tree, loved by the Lord;
and Jesus galivanting on Galilee,
dishing out loaves and fishes
and pinned on Golgotha like a
mutilated moth: and these
were the tales that fuelled my fancy,
gave me a grammar of plots
and protagonists with which
to bejewel my world.

Remembrance

In the Point we called our cenotaph
simply "The Monument," and etched
in stolid stone were the names
of long-ago battles
too brutal to be celebrated,
and on the slim plinth
a roll-call of those
who gave their all for the king
of a far country, and atop
this edifice of remembrance
the bust of an unknown soldier
stares out over the town,
looking lonely and unanointed.

Beyond Hope

If there were a god dispensing
kudos and brickbats,
I could curse him for letting Tom die,
but I am not a man
of belief in matters beyond
hope, and so my grief
must bleed leeward to brood
in the bone, and my cries for relief
find no home,
here or in Heaven.

When I Was Young Enough

When I was young enough
to know better and easy
in my bones, I grew like a
slow rose in luminous
light and swung from season
to season unfettered by Time
or its baleful buffeting, and I spent
my days grazing the grass
of Grandfather's lawn as green
as the glens of Eden, where dandelions
danced like spun suns,
hedged by lilacs hung
lavender in loose profusion,
and I sampled the dappled shade
of Manitoba maples and the breezes
that blew effusive through them,
and when I ventured to the edge
of anywhere, a lake appeared
so blue the sky would blush –
and these were the gist of the similes
that teemed inside me and sought
solace in the pulsing of my poems.

The Knack

Into a May morning
and the village that spawned me
where the sun rose over
First Bush like a blown
bloom and lacquered the streets
with a soothing luminosity,
I strode – like Adam greeting
God at the gates of Eden,
my body a womb for words
and their slow explosions, my head
a-burst with bardic dreams,
and I plumbed the tillage of my town
for the prescience of a poem
or the knowing flow of an ode,
certain I was born with the knack.

Ode

In my town poems grew
on trees like apples from the orchards
of Eden, nurtured by a consenting
sun and ripe for plucking
by the first apprentice bard
to feel the surge of a word
he couldn't define or a rhythm
needing a rhyme to capture
a cadence, and I felt blessed
to be a budding balladeer
among my people and tuck
their hopes and happiness in the
throes of an ode.

Festooned

Missus Bray dreamed
of blooms in her garden,
festooned with flowers of every
ilk, and when the sun
came up, it soothed
the day's bouquets as soft
as any satin or silk,
and she bid them bask in the
purview of her praise,
and when night came down,
she dreamed again of daisies
and daffodils in their delight
and let her widowed heart
teem.

The Breath in the Breeze

I took an afternoon to search
for the gist of things, like the
breath that breathes in the breeze
or the light that lurks in a bloom
just stunned by the sun
or the reason for the moon's being
luminous or who groomed
the stars' ept architecture
or the secret behind the precise
cycling of the seasons, and when
I find it, here or at home,
I'm going to put it in the
pristine pistoning of a poem.

Budding

As I grazed the Parnassian pastures
of Grandfather's lawn,
I was pursued by bardic dreams,
my head agog with an extravagance
of stanzas and rhymes looking for the
chime of a couplet and rhythms
that dithered and danced, and I wanted
to ink the world and its people
in passionate pentameters
to amaze and delight: my words
unbudding, liberated by light.

Heft

Whenever we dare to love
with all the heft of our heart,
we risk the sting of rejection
or worse, the lingering longitude
of loss when the one we adore
abandons breath and being
and we are left with the hectic
reckoning of grief — but to love
is to be alive enough
to discover, curled inside,
some vulnerable version
of ourselves we would not trade
for Heaven or the world.

O What a Morning

O what a marvel is a summer
morn in the place where I was born,
when the sun blossomed above
First Bush like an over-
exposed rose and lacquered
the streets with lyrical light,
and I, sequestered in my home-
cocoon, set out
to harvest happiness in the dappled
shade of elm and oak
where infant breezes whelmed,
my head agog with bardic
bravado in quest of the perfect
phrase to amplify the iambic
dance of this daunting day,
pleased to let it fester
like a bruise in the bone before it
brightens and blooms.

Woo

Whenever we caught a pair
of dogs 'doing it' on the walk,
the girls blushed as pink
as a peony, and we just marvelled
at the conjugal apparatus
of canine wooing and dreamed
one day that we too
might give it a go – gratis.

Rhyme

My poems come from somewhere
deep within the bardic
bone, where the id dozes
in ribald repose, until
the itch to beget grips it
bidden, and words flow
into the easy iambic of an ode
or the supple couplets of a balladeer's
banter, and I've spent the better
part of a lifetime pillaging
the voluminous root of the home-
ground and the village that hatched me
whole into a world rich
with ritual and rhyme.

Instinct

I was born with in instinct for ink,
a penchant for perpetrating poetry,
and when I strode the streets
of the town that debouched me,
similes sang in the breeze
and Dylan's dactyls danced
on a dime, and I wanted to pin
my home and its people in the perfect
pincers of a poem or the slow
glow of an ode and did not
know then that the Muse
would continue her timely
transfusions for the rest of my days
and let my words, wrenched
awry, have their say.

Cradle

I've been told that even as a
toddler I was often whelmed
by an upwelling of words,
nurtured by the sing-song
thrum of the nursery rhyme
and the three-pronged plots
of Goldilocks, imprudent pigs
and Billy Goats gruff
enough to enfever my polyglot
fancy, and I sensed even then
that poems were bred out of bone
and the body in the ease of its breathing:
our lilting, infant syllables
unquelled in the cradle.

A-Dazzle

When I was young enough
to unremember, my world
was composed of Grandfather's
yard, hemmed in by hedges
where lilacs hung in lavender
loops and roses swooned
on the arch of their arbour, and each
bloom sunned itself
singular, each petal
its own proud poem,
and something instinct
in the breeze trembling between
the leaves brought me up-
right to the brink of seeing:
and all was then a-dazzle.

Lost

Missus Bradley stood
on her front stoop, blinked
the sun's ink from her eyes
and uttered a cry that blossomed
from her bones and soared up
through the throttle of her throat
and out to the furthest ear
in the titillated town, and there was
the shudder of shame in it
and a yearning for something
smitten she had long-ago
lost.

Pouch

On a mid-May morning
when I was just young
enough, I debouched onto
the dew-gilded grass of Grand-
father's lawn, hugged
by hedges a-lust with lilacs,
limned by light and seasoned
in the breeze tugging at the leaves,
and something like a word
urged itself upward,
like the essence of the day,
and I tucked it into the pouch
of a poem.

Far to Go

On this Summer's day
an hour before the dark
devours it, my lake is as blue
as the Heaven that holds it
and we swim gingerly into the
soft surround, our bodies
thin-skinned, bloodless
with buoyancy, unhinged
from its hunger, and way out
where the heat-haze hovers,
a sun hesitates on the horizon
like a moon too bruised to fall,
and we know we all have far
to go.

Scenery

When God purloined a random
rib from Adam and confected
Eve, the tupless couple
passed their days, in feckless
tandem, admiring the scenery
until Eve, with an appetite
for apples and a gnaw for knowing,
took a bite, and Adam, new
to wooing, bit bigger,
as chuffed as a second banana
chewing the scenery.

Plots and Perils

I teethed on Bible stories:
Adam and Eve in the Garden
where everything grew but love
and sex was unacceptable;
Samson with his impeccable coif
that Delilah bisected, then tittered
as the temple unresurrected
around him; Abednego
toasting his toes in the fiery
furnace; Daniel lounging
with lions as limpid as lambs;
Moses in the bulrushes,
who pulled down the pillar
of fire to light the way
through a severed sea;
Job: who suffered boils
and sores and begged for more;
Joshua and his jolly jaunt
to the portals of Paradise;
and Jesus who ambled with ease
on Galilee, rolled a rock away
and rose from the dead like a
hallowed Houdini— and these
were the plots and perils I carried
with me like an embarking bard
and I let them breed in my genes.

The Morning of the World

Tom and I walking
the woods that hug our lake
in scented cedar and white-
barked birch, as if
the waters were too blue
to be unloosed, and where
moss dosses on the north
side of trees and butterflies
stutter on the breath of the breeze
and jays with cummerbunds
bicker like vexed vicars
and a Massassauga slithers
hither and yon with a shake
of its tinfoil tail
and dragonflies, helium-
winged, prance with aplomb,
and down in the swamp bull-
frogs thrum their melodious
monologue, and in walking
these elemental desmesnes
something in us is born
anew, our souls reawakened
in the morning of the world.

Where Love Lives

With a nod to Emily D

When God took your breath
away and let your body
be, I cursed Him and a universe
where Death and his dam, Mortality,
gamble our chances agley,
 but with the coming of each
forgiving dawn, love
lives on.

Flock

The Widow Bray prayed
for rain to rinse the April
bulbs of her hyacinths
and for sunlight to boost them
into bloom, and she found room
in her layman's heart for both
God and her garden, certain
that what He deemed arable
would propagate and all
her flowered flock come
home to roost.

Ruptured

God, the Great Poetaster,
created Earth on a seven-
day spree, but first
He practiced on Paradise,
messed up some dust
and adumbrated Adam,
then, playing the odds,
He fashioned Eve and bade her
keep her beauty bashful,
but lust for the Tree Forbidden
upset the apple-cart,
and the Royal Rhymster hastened
to rid his prize production
of the ruptured couple.

Kingdom Come

We had only one murder
in the Point, in the years where I grew
bemused: young Lumley,
beguiled by the girl next door,
already betrothed to another,
refused to take her no
for an answer and, despite
a tumult of tears, girded
his loins, borrowed his brother's
gun and blew her brains
to Kingdom Come.

Blinding

Missus Bradley wandered
her clapboard abode,
wondering what room
she was in, and when nothing
came to mind, stood
staring from her front stoop
under a sun that bloomed
too blinding for the eye
and, her thoughts thickening,
wondered what'd happened
to the sky.

Eight for Anne
In loving memory

Linked

I wake: disappointed
that I did not dream you alive
and loving in this moonlit
room, where our bodies once
blended in illicit felicity,
and I want so much to reprise
that tenderness of touch,
that cozy camaraderie
of lovers easy in the other's
eye, at home in our linked
history, but I find I'm not
exempt from heartbreak,
lost in a cone of aloneness
and left with a grief that burns
like a blister on the bone.

Illume

With a nod to Dylan Thomas

I wake and our room is illumed
by moonlight soothing
the counterpane where we lay
entangled by touch, and for
a moment I choose to forget
this is a dream and you
have gone where love is never
enough, and I am left
marooned in my own aloneness
like a loon without a lake
with my bereavement pain
throbbing like a bruise burrowed
in the bone, and doomed to remember
how we once embraced
like young gods in their begetting,
as if Death held no
dominion and all sins
were forgiven in the furious fusion
of flesh.

Autumn Morning: 1960

Whenever I feel the need
to ease the grip of my grief,
I dream of that October
morning when you pulled up
to the curb in your sleek Beetle
and stepped out like Cleopatra
debouching from her barge,
the breeze making a halo
of your hair, your lips a limned
ellipse, your eyes as lively
as agates in a toddler's palm
and as blue as the sky is deep,
and I knew for the first time
that a smile could calm the churning
chambers of a heart – and such
a remembrance, for a moment,
soothes a bereavement pain
that stings like a cinder smouldering
in the bone.

Far Out

If you were alive again,
I would take you by the hand
and stroll you barefoot through the
slow rollers of the Lake
that once held me, toddling,
in its chaste embrace, and you
would salute the summering sun,
soothing in the dunes, older
than Methuselah's dam
and oozing hoarded heat,
while above us, herring-gulls
sting the breeze with pied
cries, and hunger and, far out,
other worlds glorify
their gods and await our arrival

Winnowed

You had a smile that set
the roses in the window aglow
and you beguiled with a beauty
no bard would call Venusian,
but rather one that bloomed
in the bone, enthusing upward
through the horizon of the eyes
in wry amusement at a world
obsessed with the female's furrowed
flesh, but with me it was love
at first sight with a dozen
yellow roses begetting
beauty in a window winnowed
by light.

Gloaming

You always had the homing
instinct, like the puffin idling
to the island of its birth or a dove
to the comfort of its cote or a pea—
hen feathering her brood
with a warm-winged love,
and you were ever tethered
to the children you bore and imbued,
and I cherished you for them – and now
that you have gone to the brink
and beyond, I have those gentle,
mothering gestures to remember
and the smile that lit your eyes
like a gilded rose aglow
in the gloaming.

Serendipity

I wake from a dream of you
in my arms once again,
letting our bodies be,
as they were when our love was young
and each moon-soothed
evening thereafter we renewed
the teeming of its touch
and its serendipity of soul,
and I wanted so much
to keep you free from all
harm, from the fretful fury
of a world where the gods demur
and deny, and a love like ours
would falter and die, but we beat
the odds for fifty-seven years
of loving and the lyric of laughter.

Lissome

Under the supple strumming
of stars and a moon enthused
with its own galactic glow
and the susurration of rollers
rinsing the shore, we make
lissome, languid love
as if we were the first
couple on Earth in the blush
of its beginning, and in the
moon-endued dark
I swear to love you from here
to Heaven and back.

Sixteen for Tom

In Loving Memory

Peaceful

They say the grave is a peaceful
place, where sleepers lie
in dreamless ease and bravely
count the hours till Time
turns into Eternity and the soul
releases like a disembodied
god and sings halleluiahs
to the Heavens, and if you had
to die with your life still
in the bud, I am comforted
for a moment by such ethereal
thoughts, alone with what
is left of a grief that throbs
like a bobbin in the blood.

Delirium

O Tom! There is no
pain like the kind that fractures
my heart whenever I think
of you unalive, somewhere
without the lithium of light
or the salve of love's solace,
and my grief breaks over me
like a tidal tantrum loosed
by the moon in oscillating
inundations, and anywhere
I turn I see your adoring
eyes and I know it's just
the delirium of dream, but I
prize it just the same
and let it stoke the wokened
locus of my loss, for when
you died, you left me bitter
in the bone, like a body embalmed.

Similes

I scoured the milkweed meadow
for the seeds of similes to sweeten
my budding verse, where butterflies
embraced the breeze like tipsy
tumblers and larks stitched
the sky with song like sopranos
on a spree and rumpled pods
exposed their silken insides
like lovers lanced by lust
and dragonflies danced
like prim pas-de-deux
and bulrushes shook
their shaggy heads like Rapunzel
unmuzzling her luscious
locks and adders wove
their warp and woof like a
spinster worrying her wheel,
and when my walk was through
I had tropes enough for an
eclectic epic dedicated
to you.

Immaculate

How many times since you
left me for the sloe abode
of the grave have I dreamt you alive
again in this room
where we talked books and the perils
of poetry that harrows the heart?
And you were wise enough
to parse my fledgling efforts
with the tact of a gentle juror
and a smile that incandesced
your eyes and reassured the world
that love is what shines through us
like the immaculate bones of a poem

A Kind of Joy

In the midst of my grief, the thought
of your elfin grin blooms
in my mind, and soothes, and a
kind of joy wells up
when I remember I had you
whole and aloft for thirty
years and more, and we kept
room in our hearts for a love
beyond the reach of belief,
and O my beautiful boy!
you have settled softly into my soul.

Glee

Some nights are made
for remembrance, like the one
when we tobogganed on Gibbon's
infant hill in the moon-
hued dark, when you were just
five and we found ourselves
tucked as tight as twins
limned in the womb — against
our lively glide and the breeze
your cheeks stirred amid
winnowing "whees!" as gravity
gave way and we whistled
beyond its wistful grip until
we bottomed out like breath
from a balloon, dazzled by our own
delight, agog with glee.

Autumnal Wind

When the wind hums autumnal,
Earth denies the dying:
leaves forgo their green
sheen for a crimson ignition
and melons mellow in the fields,
plumped by the last licks
of a lapsing sun, and butternut
seethes with seed and robins
fatten and feather in time
for their continental cruise
and orchards hang heavy
with newly juiced fruit
and roses doze like dowagers
in final flourish, and all
things natural, however
hard they may have tried,
like you, were unprepared
to die.

Something of Winter

There was something of Winter in you,
not the nip and niggle
of cold that comes creeping
when the sun sallies south,
but a sense of what needs to be
protected, like Summer's seeds
shrinking into themselves
to preserve their hoarded heat,
or bulbs that doze in the frozen
ground and wait for April's
lancing light or a maple's
sap that wriggles free
of leaves and rallies to the root,
and you let me glimpse
that secret seed from time
to time with a glint in your eye
that seemed to say, "That
is why we love," and I felt
blessed to be in your presence,
sharing that discreet piece
of your soul, which will never
die, even now that you
have gone to your grave
and left me less than whole.

More than Broken

Death has no grievance
against the living, no more
than the dark complain of the
lancing of light or the moon
cavil about competition
from the architecture of the stars
or a breeze resent the trees
that squeeze it pleasing: Death
simply plays its lethal
game with a random ruthlessness
and a predilection for victims
in the full flowering of their years,
in the certain surging of their powers,
and when your last breath
abandoned your body (with so much
unspoken between us)
I found myself alone
with the pain of your gleeless going,
like a blight blackening in the bone,
my heart more than broken.

Sally

How many hours did we dally
in that book-bloomed room,
discussing the power of poetry
to move us beyond the centering
self to something that would
startle the stars, embolden
the breath of our being, and leave us
open to love's soothing
lunacy? And when our eyes,
lit with literature's illume,
met, we smiled and let
our souls sally.

All the Days

I loved you most in the morning
when sunlight gilded the grass
and dappled the dew, and a breeze,
derelict from the dawn, breathed
easy in the maples and rippled
the face of the Lake like shook silk
and a robin's song throbbed
in his throat –
and I loved you most in the afternoon
when the sun snoozed in a high
sky and breezes blew
as if they mattered and larks
sent their serenades meandering
over meadows, and rollers,
freshening in the Lake, consoled
the nearest shore –
and I loved you most in the evening
when the breeze subtled and the moon
marinated the stars and induced
a drifting of dream, and children
played hide-and-seek,
charmed by the dark –
I loved you then and all
the days before, and even
though you've gone, I love you
even more.

Lexicon

My poems arise like geysers
from some burrow abiding
in the bone or, when the Muse
is muted, like a slow budding
in the blood, but gushing or aglow
they are rooted in the kind of love
you brought to me from the
morning you were born and sought
my adoring eyes and all
the days of our doting dalliance,
until you sallied astray,
and so it is I pen
these lines, looted from the lexicon
and seasoned in my genes, to say
again how much you've sanctified
my life.

Radiant

I wake from a dream of you
alive and loving, with a smile
in your eyes as mellow as moon-
light strumming the stars,
but the room is soon emptied
of everything but me and my grief,
throbbing like a burr in the blood,
but when your face swims
again into view, I am
unbenumbed and grateful
for such illicit visitations
and the soothing maneuvres of the dreams
that nourish my nights, heal
my heart and bring you back:
radiant and limned by light.

Rhythms

Once again we find
ourselves in this nurturing
nook, a-bloom with books
and talk of matters literary,
and I remark that you
have been my Muse, an earnest
ear for my iambic patter
and a gentle jurist when the
need arose, and it's only
you who knows the loneliness
of the ceaseless search for the
immaculate word, the moiling
for meaning just beyond
the semblance of sense or the bardic
mind seething with simile,
and what a joy to sit here
with you in this room and its
rarefied rhythms, ruminate,
and be.

Sweat

How many Saturday mornings
with the sun still raw on the
horizon, did we pack your pads
and pouches into the maw
of your hockey-bag and head
for some drafty rink
where the stink of last week's
sweat wafted and whetted
and you armoured yourself
like a gladiator getting fitted
for the lions, and I watched in awe
as the big-boned lug
of your body floated over the
ice like an enthusiastic swan
adrift from the grip of gravity
and polishing a pond? And it is
just such a memory
I call upon to ease
my lonely grief that tugs
like a tunour a-burst in the bone.

Eyrie

You loved the little room
of your mother's womb so much
you decided to linger a day
or two longer in that sea-
easing surround, before
the lurching of your birth brought you
upright in the ambient air
with your elfin grin intact
and eyes as blue as moonstones
limned by light, and so
it was no surprise twenty
years on to find you and I
in our arable eyrie, where books
bloomed like heather aglow
in a glen, and you knew even then
that poetry is the soul singing
solo to itself.

Don Gutteridge was born in Sarnia and raised in the nearby village of Point Edward. He taught High School English for seven years, later becoming a Professor in the Faculty of Education at Western University, where he is now Professor Emeritus. He is the author of more than seventy books: poetry, fiction and scholarly works in pedagogical theory and practice. He has published twenty-two novels, including the twelve-volume Marc Edwards mystery series, and forty books of poetry, one of which, Coppermine, was short-listed for the 1973 Governor-General's Award. In 1970 he won the UWO President's Medal for the best periodical poem of that year, "Death at Quebec."

Don lives in London, Ontario.

To listen to interviews with the author, go to: http://thereandthen.podbean.com.

Visit his website at dongutteridgewriter.com.

Email address: dongutteridge37@gmail.com.